Burying My Corpse: Letting Go of a Dead Relationship

by: Ruth Agbolosoo

Vol. 1 The Beginning of the End

Burying My Corpse:
Letting Go of a Dead Relationship
Volume 1

Copyright 2021 - 2023 by Ruth Agbolosoo

All rights reserved.

No part of this book or subsequent volumes, may be reproduced or utilized in any form or by any means, electronic or mechanical, including photocopying and recording, or by any information storage and retrieval system, without permission in writing from the author.

Praise for Burying My Corpse

"I was in tears." Ana

"I love your writing style." Trellanie

"I love this!" "The imagery and journey are so SPOT ON!!! I feel like I am in there with you." Elizabeth

"Deeep. Very very deep. Very interesting." "So many people will want a copy. Especially folks who are broken because of failed marriages." Kerone

Other Books by Ruth Agbolosoo

Why Get Started Investing Today?
To Grow Your Money Faster
(E-book available on Amazon)

Burying My Corpse:
Letting Go of a Dead Relationship Vol. 2
(Coming Soon)

Dedication

This book is dedicated to my children. Life has not been easy but Yahweh (God) is good. He gifted me with you all because he knew I'd need the strength and motivation to make the changes necessary to catapult me into my destiny. The opportunity to be your mother has been my greatest joy and accomplishment.

I also dedicate this book to my mother who taught me about true strength and has always supported me.

Acknowledgements

"No man is an island. No man stands alone." That's the phrase that comes to my mind when I think of all the people in my life who helped me to get to where I am on this journey. You see, I have several books that have not been published. It took a lot for me to actually go through with this process. I have had many sleepless nights. I also had a lot of anxiety about sharing openly about my life, particularly my inner thoughts.

I want to first acknowledge my Lord and Savior Yashua the Messiah. You may call him Jesus and others may call Him by another name or alliteration. However, without Him none of this would be possible. As a woman of faith in Yahweh (God), I wrestled for a long time with the words that I knew to be true. "God hates divorce" (Malachi 2:16). My desire has always been to please my father by living an upright life. But, I've made so many mistakes. Some I'm willing to share openly and some, not really. I'm not perfect but He has shown me His love in many ways and has accepted me as His child. He provided me with the peace I needed to embark on this journey. I'm grateful!

Next, I wanted to acknowledge one of my best friends, Amanda. We've gone through a lot of ups and downs but she has always been a great friend to me. When I felt I was on sinking sand, she held me up. She gave me gentle reminders that I deserved better. Amanda, I was listening and I'm grateful for your love and support.

I want to thank my therapist Ann, who was the first person that I decided to share my book with. At that time, it wasn't really a book but rather, a journal. She empowered me to share my thoughts with others. I am grateful that I have her in my life. She has really helped me sort through my feelings.

I also want to acknowledge the wonderful ladies who read my book when it was still rough and gave me pointers and encouragement along the way. Thank you Ana, Trellanie, and Elizabeth. I appreciate you taking out the time to assist me with this. Ana, thank you for expressing your heart in the foreword.

Lastly, I want to acknowledge my designer and friend, Taneil. Not only have you worked with me diligently on my projects including this book, but you have been a sounding board and an encourager to me. I'm so grateful to you.

Foreword

Reading this book, I found this not to be a metaphor, but a reality. Though my marriage didn't end in a divorce, my husband died on December 2, 2015, I connected with so much of what the author speaks of; that one must deal with the cessation of a relationship - one must deal with a death.

Two words leaped out in front of me when I completed the reading:
selah and shema.

I love the Hebrew language. It is an amazing language of action; the tongue of "to do". Words bear weight when they command an action to be accomplished through sentences.

Shema means, "hear", "listen". I heard the sadness, vulnerability, regret; the raw, and exposed. The risk and the reluctance.

Selah is a word in Hebrew that means, to pause; to consider. Ms. Agbolosoo carefully and delicately shares these thoughts and feelings with us for she knows now is the time that all who have experienced the same feelings in a divorce need to face the reality of it; pause and reflect in their own way. She's evidently painted not just the tragedies but the beauty within her marriage. That is why it was hard to let go. She wants all who have gone through this similar turmoil to hear her story, listen, and connect with their own hearts and reflect; not just to stop here alone, but to decide and choose what is best for themselves.

Ana Amandula M Garcia

Introduction

    This book is highly metaphorical. Using metaphors helped me with conceptualizing my situation, as I was able to fully explore the major themes in this book; the notion of holding on to a dead relationship and convincing myself to let go.

    Before I made the decision to write this, my head was spinning. I was having panic attacks and didn't know what to do with myself. Then I decided to take charge. I pulled myself together, took a deep breath, grabbed a notebook and pen, and decided to write from my heart.

During the process, I felt empowered. It really helped me release my emotions and start to heal. Making the decision to get a divorce was huge, and a very emotional time. Aside from my weekly therapy sessions, with my lovely therapist Ann, I needed a way to process my feelings and convince myself to keep going.

This book was written as another form of therapy. It helped me process the grief and the internal struggle related to going through the process of the divorce. It is the first volume in a series about my journey through the divorce process. Volume one describes the internal turmoil during the phase right after the paperwork was filed. Those were the moments of inner dialogue when I realized that I took action and now change was inevitable.

Not enough people talk about the emotional rollercoaster one goes through after making the decision to get a divorce. There are moments of absolute despair and moments of self-satisfaction. There are other feelings in between, including guilt and fear.

Introduction

There were also a lot of questions in my head as I struggled against the temptation to second-guess myself and cancel the divorce. I had done that before and it didn't serve me well. It just delayed the inevitable. If anything good came out of changing my mind and canceling the divorce, it was that I gained clarity about the situation and knew that my marriage wasn't going to work out.

If you are contemplating divorce, this phase is very tough, yet it is rarely mentioned. This is a great time to surround yourself with positive support. If you have been divorced, I believe you may be able to relate to this.

Sharing my experience was not easy but I knew it was necessary.

My hope is to bring awareness about what goes on internally during this phase, so others can be supportive of their loved ones going through a divorce, and those contemplating divorce will be prepared.

I also hope that more people will talk about this phase of the divorce process so the feelings involved are normalized and people don't feel so isolated. Finally, I hope that it provides a sense of healing and validation for all who read it. I will take you with me in subsequent volumes as I walk through the other phases of the divorce process. Thank you for reading this expression from my heart.

Shock and Denial

I think I understand why some people live with a deceased loved one in their house. I've heard of a few cases over my lifetime. It's so creepy to hear about. I have thought to myself, "He must be crazy. I could never live with a dead person in the house." It's unthinkable and unimaginable. Only a depraved person could do that. How is it even possible? Well, I think I know why and how that happens based on my experience. It comes down to shock and denial. First, he or she is shocked that the person is dead. Then, he or she is in denial about it. He or she could not be gone. He or she can't leave me. He or she didn't leave me. At least if he or she stays here, I will be okay. Even if he or she cannot talk or walk or do anything, that's better than being alone.

Those may be some thoughts one ponders on when faced with such a grave situation. The voiceless and actionless body is better than having no one at all or not seeing him or her again. It is so impossible to let go. Letting go of what once was, is so painful. So instead, he or she may convince him or herself that the person is not dead. Accepting reality is like volunteering to stand in front of a firing squad. You're pretty much inviting the inevitable pain and suffering that is imminent.

For a long time, that was my attitude towards my marriage. When my marriage "died", I didn't want to let go. I was in shock that it didn't work out. It was supposed to last forever. All of my dreams of what my marriage could and would look like slowly faded away. I couldn't believe it. "How could this have happened to me?" It was like reliving a scene from a bad dream. I wanted to wake up and see that things were just as they should be. I wanted happily ever after. I was sure that I would be the wife of a doting husband. We would raise our sweet little children together. My husband and I would take vacations together and grow old together.

We didn't get the dream house yet. We didn't get the rental properties for our children. What happened to the legacy we wanted to build? What happened to the hope that I'd have a marriage that would sustain a lifetime of ups and downs like my parents? I can't believe my marriage ended up being like something out of a TLC movie, a tear-jerker with lots of shocking, suspenseful moments. I can't believe it ended the way it did...

I was in denial. I knew my marriage was dead but I didn't want to face the reality of what that actually entailed. It had been lifeless for so long. It lacked the vital signs of a thriving marriage. There was no nurturing, friendship, trust, care, and hope for a bright future. Little by little the dreams of a young couple started fading fast and the reality that things were on a quick downward slope came into view. It seemed as though the bond that held it together was strong but that was not the case. It was being held together by an adhesive that was low-grade. It was a farce. Only those with an insider's view knew that. Yet, I told myself things like, "No. It's not over." "I can make this work. I just have to figure out how." "Maybe if I pray harder." "Maybe if I am more friendly or helpful, I can revive it." "It's not dead yet. I see a little something that with the right treatment can revive this marriage and even make it better than it ever was."

Facing the Truth

However, it was already dead. It was a picture of a marriage. It was a wide smile caught in a brief photo op. To the onlooker, it looked as if it was real. Two people who look beautiful together with beautiful children, a beautiful house, and nice things on social media always call for "#goals". Unfortunately, my marriage was just a label and a part of my identity. I was someone's wife. I had a husband and sometimes a lover. I had held on to this dead marriage for several years. At times, I was hopeful that it would be resurrected. I doted on it. I planned for it. I tried to make it look pretty. I dressed it up and made it a continued priority. I made sure it smelled good enough to convince myself that it wasn't actually dead.

All the while, it sat there - listless. It provided nothing that my soul truly needed. It didn't provide the healing and love that my soul was yearning for. I didn't have a confidant to share my problems and secrets with. I kept them to myself. I spoke, yet only the air heard me. There was no one to respond to my concerns or jubilations. No one to celebrate my wins or tend to my wounds. I slept in a cold bed that was void of comfort. There was no one to keep me warm at night, no one to kiss me on my forehead and tell me that things were going to be okay, and no one to defend me when life was throwing several darts at me.

Sweet Memories

My bed was riddled with memories of cuddles, hot lovemaking, whispers of pillow talk, and midnight prayers. The memories of sunlit mornings, watching a naked body relaxed in the bed beside me, remembering what happened a few hours before with a smile on my face, often filled my head. Visions of that feeling of warmth, as that body rolled over to me, caressing or spooning me, would give me a warm and fuzzy feeling. I even daydreamed about those early morning sites of a naked body getting ready for work as I admired every curve and detail of each part. It was fully exposed to me. It tantalized me, as I wished it was still night and there was more time to embrace it.

But, all I was left with was just memories. Except for the title, label, and notions, my marriage was dead. No amount of memories, good wishes, tingling sensations in my toes, or even prayers could resurrect it. But still, I held onto it. It was as if I had made a decision that a dead marriage was better than no marriage at all. It was though it didn't matter anymore. I was used to the corpse being around.

The Stages of Death

After a while, it didn't smell so bad. I didn't look at it all the time, so the withered skin and protruding bones bothered me less and less. The scraggly hairs and discoloration were frightening at times, but I kept busy and did not focus on those things.

Little by little decomposition set in, and the listless body looked less and less like the marriage I had once cherished. I first realized that it was dead when autolysis set in. The lack of oxygen, in the form of love, caused it to destroy itself. It was such a toxic environment. Every effort made to salvage it caused even more damage. Then, finally, it went into rigor mortis. That's when the real shift happened and every effort made to revive it was in vain. It started to stink. It started to discolor and swell. I could see that this rapid change was taking place. However, as I watched it begin to lose its mass and start to shrivel, I held on. There were no kind words spoken. There were no nice gestures to be received. Eventually, a marriage that I once treasured became a skeleton. It had no substance or vigor. There wasn't anything left there to be called a marriage. The only thing that existed was documentation. Legal papers identified it as living though the reality was far from that.

Empty Hope

I wanted things to be better. I had hoped that they would improve but it was too late. I asked myself, "What if it comes back to life?" I didn't want to bury it just in case. I had heard of stories where people were pronounced dead and then were discovered alive during the funeral or even afterward. I really couldn't let that happen. I had to make a valiant effort to make sure that there were no vital signs.

Every night I went to bed in despair and woke up and kissed it good morning. I held onto the fact that it was mine. No one could take it from me. "I am a wife." "I am a spouse." My identity was shaky but as long as I didn't let go of that corpse, I could keep my identity intact.

After a while, my marriage was hard to recognize. It looked very different that I didn't think I really wanted it anymore. I battled with that part of me that remembered the youthful playtimes, the hot steamy lovemaking, the cuddles, the passionate kisses, laughter, and date nights. That part of me would remember the talks about our future plans, the two-seater car we'd have when our children were grown and gone, the large home we wanted to buy, the trips we planned to take, and gracefully growing old together.

Wrestling with Guilt

Coincidentally, that part of me was also the part that kept making me feel guilty whenever I wanted to let it go. She made me feel like a failure. "You couldn't even keep a man." She would say. She convinced me that everyone is going to blame me for the marriage not working out. She questioned my belief in God. She made me feel like I was giving up too early. She made me feel like I had not explored every possibility. "Maybe you should try this." "Maybe you should try that." She threw out so many suggestions. She reminded me that I would be the only one in my friend group that is divorced as if I didn't feel isolated enough.

She made me feel as though I was the one at fault for abandoning my marriage and leaving my lonely husband all alone without anyone to love him. She made me feel like a homewrecker. Now my children would not have mom and dad together. She questioned whether I was really in an abusive relationship. If I were more cooperative he would not have yelled or put his hands on me. He had a right to cut me off from the Internet and TV. He had a right to cut off the utilities. I had pushed him to do it. If I had been less stubborn and more supportive, he would have been a wonderful husband to me. He was just trying to teach me a lesson. He wanted me to understand his sacrifices for our family and that he didn't want to do it alone. He needed more support and a wife who would obey and not give him a hard time. She also made me feel guilty for my children's poor image of marriage. She really knows how to pour on the guilt, doesn't she? She even blamed me for getting married in the first place, but that's a story for another time. Well, now I am fighting with that side of me on a regular basis. I know some of what she says may have some sliver of truth but I think it is time. As a matter of fact, I know it is time. I need to let go.

Burying My Corpse - Vol 1

There's Nothing Left

The corpse needs to be buried. It stinks. It's deteriorating quickly and it serves no purpose. I don't cherish my identity that much anymore. Being someone's wife and lover is not holding that much weight anymore. There is no one cherishing me. No one keeps me warm at night. No cuddles or caresses. No hot steamy lovemaking. No spooning. No midnight pillow talks. No slow hand-in-hand walks. No talks of future plans. No confidant. No friend. No late-night snacks and movie watching. There's nothing left to hold onto. Yet, it's still hard to let go. It hurts!

Burying My Corpse - Vol 1

The Process has Started

I called the coroner ("lawyer"). The paperwork is signed and sent. The marriage will be picked up soon and carted away. Part of me is confident that this is for the best but, of course, that other side is beating up on me. She won't let me have any peace. It's hard to focus on work or family obligations, not to mention my business. I am waiting now to see what will happen next. How will I react as the corpse is being removed? I don't know. Will I change my mind and block the door? Will I be relieved or will I start grieving all over again? Only time will tell.

In the meantime, I still have this dead thing in my possession. I'm trying not to look at it. But of course, I have to glance at it every now and then. It's hard not to. Yes, I'm crying because I know it's going away soon. I'm hoping to at least be able to act and look "normal" when that time comes. I mean, isn't that what everyone does? I don't know. I don't even know what "normal" is. I just know I can't let everyone know what I'm going through. I can't let them know I just got rid of my corpse. I really hope when it's gone I can keep it together. Please, God! Help me to keep it together!

About the Author

Ruth Agbolosoo is the Founder and CEO of Women's Financial Empowerment Group which is the Financial Coaching and Financial Consulting arm of RuthG Consulting. Ruth is a financial empowerment coach with a passion for promoting financial literacy among women and empowering them to achieve their financial goals.

Ruth successfully managed a household on limited funds for a long period of time using the financial principles she learned and teaches to her clients. Drawing from her background in counseling, she encourages self-love, positivity, and productivity using her various social media platforms including Facebook and her YouTube channel, Women's Financial Empowerment Group (name on both).

Ruth's public speaking engagements have included topics related to personal finance, business finance and development, parenting, homeschooling, and domestic violence related issues.

Ruth received her Master's degree in Marriage and Family Therapy from Liberty University and holds a Bachelor's degree in Psychology. Ruth lives in the Midwest and provides care for her mother and three youngest children.

For media inquiries, speaking engagements, and PR please email her at
AWomensFinancialEmpowerment@gmail.com.

www.ingramcontent.com/pod-product-compliance
Lightning Source LLC
Chambersburg PA
CBHW020916080526
44589CB00011B/615